MW00769860

I'm Down with You

An Inspired Journey

JAGATJOTI S. KHALSA WITH DARREN SETTER
FOREWORD BY ANTHONY SHRIVER

The Other Person is You { *foundation* }
3144 NE 49th Avenue
Portland, OR 97213
(503) 564-8784
www.theotherpersonisyou.org

Printed in USA

Publisher: The Other Person is You {*foundation*}
ISBN: 978-0-615-35731-7
Library of Congress Control Number: 2010905700

"There would not be stereotypes if people kept their curiosity."

~Inspired 5th Grader, Opal School

The Journey

By Jagatjoti S. Khalsa

One year ago I embarked on an inspired journey to photograph and share the beauty, radiance and extraordinary love of the Down syndrome community. One of the interesting components of my journey was my reason for beginning it. Since I was a little boy (and continuing to this day), when someone with Down syndrome crossed my path I was faced with an overall feeling of knowingness, lovingness and acceptance. In that moment, I was left experiencing all the stuff that makes someone with Down syndrome great. I was left without judgment. I was living in the moment. I felt more accepting of myself, experiencing a warm rush of love. I felt all this but I had never had a personal experience.

One day while out for a walk I watched a young man with Down syndrome and his image would not leave my mind. The next morning I remembered this man and wished I would have walked up to him and said, "Hey, I'm down with you." I chuckled at the idea but thought it sounded like a great title for a book. I went to my computer and wrote the following.

'We all struggle to find balance in our lives. We want peace of mind, a sense of calm, the ability to restore and to see the good in all, to suspend judgment, to love unconditionally and feel worthwhile.

Many people spend years pouring through self-help books, attending seminars, listening to audio tapes and praying by their bedsides for help. They struggle with the maya of their minds overtaking them and layer this condition about themselves, the judgment of an army of men weighing down on them, measuring their value based on some hierarchy of looks, talents, wealth or a host of other worldly things. Yet ironically, there already exists a model of emotional contentment and spiritual perfection – one that has been dismissed as aberrant, pitiful and flawed by those without sight or awareness. Within it we find the perfect heart to employ, a life of humble self-love and appreciation and the unconditional kindness that exemplifies the same boundary-less map we are all taught that God offers. It does not require us to journey to the top of a mountain or the pulpit of a temple, or to wear costumes, change our manner of expression or prostrate ourselves. It just requires us to be conscious and aware in the moment.'

We hope you enjoy these sacred images of true and unconditional love. If you are looking for quiet heroes who shoot arrows of love across the bow each time they speak or take a simple breath, you are in for a treat. Revel in the discovery of a piece of yourself through their eyes. Bow your head in recognition of this sacred discovery. By God's grace you have stumbled upon real people, made of flesh and blood, who represent everything you have set your prayers toward. We do not need to look solely toward Christ, Buddha, Mohammed, Krishna or any other religious figure for this experience. We can look into their gentle, joyous eyes. The eyes of grace. The eyes of acceptance. The eyes that bring our souls to the very seed of life, *love*. Sit with these images, take a deep breath and experience what I have known since I was a child – the warm flood of God's love and grace bathing you in the nectar of his perfect creation.

OLIVIA & MOM

Olivia has this amazing way of looking at people, like she is looking into your soul. I've never seen anything like it with any other child. She is mesmerized by people and the effect it has on them is unreal! I melted the first time she truly looked at me when she was just two-days-old.

Foreword

By Anthony Shriver, Founder of Best Buddies

It was just yesterday that I received a note from a new parent of a baby with Down syndrome. The father of the child was a college friend and had joined Best Buddies while a student, almost 20 years ago, with no connection to the population. He knew nothing about Down syndrome. Eventually he became one of the best leaders that Best Buddies has ever had at the college level and he has stayed involved.

He joined our board, raised money and continues to advocate for all of our volunteers for no other reason than his gut belief that all people are children of God and God has placed each of us on the planet to spread and share his message.

My friend and Best Buddies advocate welcomed a new baby into this world – and that baby has Down syndrome. What are the chances of that happening?

It shows me that life always works in mysterious ways, and we should never forget that there is a plan for each of us. We are exactly where we should be for a reason that we might not understand.

My college friend was 110 percent ready for his gift. He has welcomed his new son with open arms, has showered him with love, and is already as proud of his child as any parent on the planet. The pictures in this book capture the faces of angels on Earth and they are the treasures of our universe. They will bring smiles and opportunity to millions of people with special needs, and we can never forget that one day your child might be that special angel, but with love, all the joy in the world will come your way.

Jennifer's Gift

By Jagatjoti S. Khalsa

Every pregnancy begins with the hopes and prayers for a healthy child – one who fits into our world, loves and lives life to it's fullest. We begin with the prayers that the very best of us, and the very best God has to offer within a child, comes to bare when a pregnancy is announced. We fall in love with this baby before we have even met them. Upon the first acknowledgement of this pregnancy, it is difficult to remember a life without this child who is on their way to filling our house with love and life.

Nothing brings hope eternal like a baby on its way.

When you feel this baby – this opportunity for love and hope – does it really matter if it is going to have an extra chromosome? Does it really matter if we know it might come in last more than first at a foot race? Does it matter whether it struggles with a second language but loves in its first so beautifully. Does it matter if it will struggle but will overcome obstacles? Does anything really matter other than soon we will hold in our hands this child?

When Jennifer learned she had a child with Down syndrome coming to join her family, she was fearful. Imagine the confusion and flood of mixed feelings. The anger, frustration, self-blaming and the feeling of the unknown which washed over her. She was not expecting any of this and she was not prepared to know how to process these feelings.

Now imagine a woman of such force, love and strength who can overcome fear, anger and self-doubt.

Do you want to know what Down syndrome does to a family and to a woman hoping her child will be perfect? Do you want to know what love looks like? Open your eyes and feel her loving gaze.

She has all of these feelings. All of them. But do you know what won? Love, like it should.

JENNIFER

Unlike my first pregnancy, I feel like I've gotten to know this baby boy even before he is born. While all of the testing after a prenatal diagnosis can be stressful, it has also been incredibly bonding. We call him "Peanut" for now, and even after his name is official, I have a feeling he'll retain the nickname, because everyone has already started to love him!

FELICIE & MOM | *When she smiles, Felicie's dimples are the most beautiful thing ever. She brings joy and happiness in our family. I like the way she observes, tries to do things on her own. I can already see she will reach her goals in the future.*

MALEA & MOM

She has one of the prettiest smiles you've ever seen. She's an avid student of American Sign Language and knows about 150 signs – way more than Mom and Dad! She has a fantastic sense of humor and can always find a way to make me smile. She is persistent and determined. She reminds me to never give up.

ILIANA & MOM

She was so full of joy. And to watch the joy brought to her mother and father's faces when they held her forced all of us to smile a grand smile.

"*The sun never says to the Earth,
'you owe me,' look what happens to a
love like that. It lights up the whole sky.*"

~ *Hafiz*

| *I look into her eyes and catch a glimpse of her soul. I can actually see how much she loves me, personally and unconditionally. It's the most perfect feeling on Earth. It's a complete love.*

A Mother's Love

By Betsy Goodwin, NDSS Founder

When my daughter Carson was first born I worried about everything – what health problems she would have, what her IQ would be, what was her life going to be like, what impact would she have on our life. I never considered in those early months, 30 years ago, *who* she would be, and that has turned out to be the most important thing of all.

Carson can only be described as a people person; she is interested in and wants to relate to everyone. She can "do" a room like a seasoned politician, expertly identifying something about each individual to compliment them about. She will usually pick a tie, jewelry, dress or hair, and I silently hope that she will pick something different when she moves on to compliment the next person within earshot.

She often hones in, with her own special radar, on fragile people and envelopes them in her warmth. She was recently at a large reception after a memorial service. One lady had come very reluctantly as she had recently completed a round of chemotherapy and was shy about her sparse hair which she had carefully arranged for the evening. Carson found her, shook her hand and complimented her on a beautiful hairdo. There were hugs, tears and laughter, and that woman stood a little straighter and prouder for the rest of the evening. At that same reception I also notice Carson sitting in a chair holding the hand of an elderly woman with Alzheimer's. What sort of sense of empathy did she have that told her such a simple gesture was needed. I am not one to believe that this is a by-product of Down syndrome – I think it is simply who she is.

Sometimes people are clearly uncomfortable around her and try to avoid meeting her. But Carson will not let them off the hook. She may only stop for a moment to compliment them, smile, shake their hand and move on, but they are the people who benefit the most from Carson's social rounds, and I can't help but hope that the next time these reluctant people meet a person with a disability, that they will be just a little more comfortable. I think it is highly likely.

So as I think back on all my worries about what my baby daughter would experience in her life – and knowing today that there are many people with Down syndrome far more accomplished than she – I just can't help but feel proud that when it is all said and done, there is nothing better I could ask of her than to be the sunny and caring person that she is.

JEREMY | *Truly a Mana in his parents life. He just sat there, present and peaceful. What a peacefulness I experienced with Jeremy and his parents.*

OLIVIA | *Olivia has this amazing way of looking at people like she is looking into your soul. I've never seen anything like it with any kid. She is mesmerized by people and the effect it has on them is unreal!*

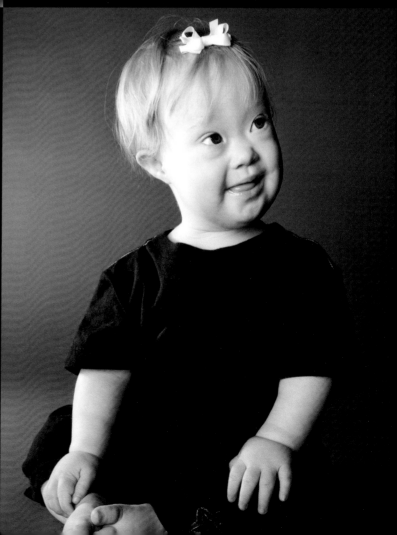

KYLIE | *A burst of energy. A burst of spirit. A burst of calmness.*

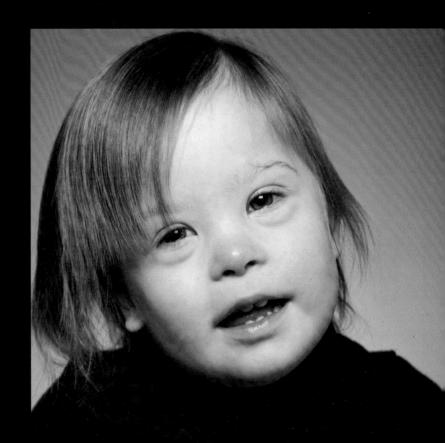

MAKENA | *Makena is a loving and extroverted individual. She has the beautiful ability to be "in the moment" every moment, seeing joy in the little things that others might not notice.*

NICOLE

Nicole always has a smile that never ends. She is very outgoing and loves to come up to you and give big hugs!!! She is very energetic and never stops. She is always such a joy to watch.

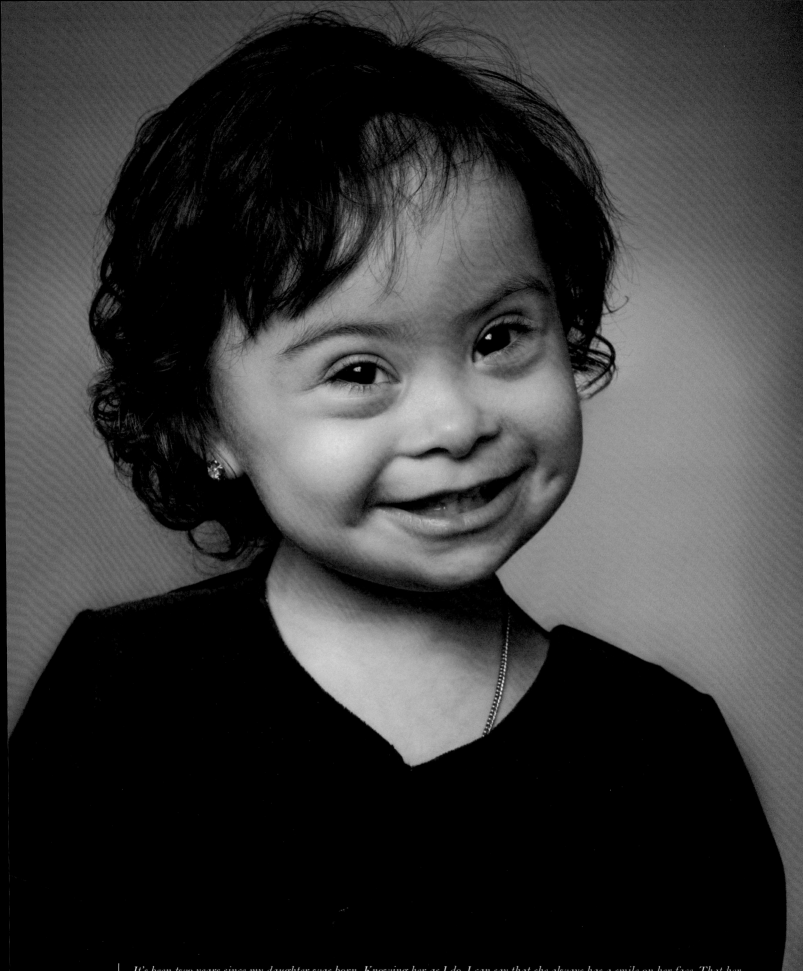

SOPHIA | *It's been two years since my daughter was born. Knowing her as I do, I can say that she always has a smile on her face. That her little arms are always open and ready to embrace me, that she comforts me by patting me on my shoulders and that she is wonderfully connected to the universe that surrounds her.*

ISAAC | *What a sweet boy.*

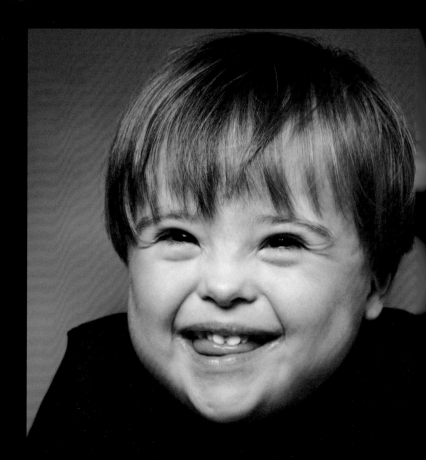

TYLER | *Tyler just has so much personality and has so much fun in everything he does. Even getting into trouble! He also has such a great sense of humor and beautiful eyes! Both of which he got from his Dad...and those are a couple of the big reasons I fell in love with him!*

THOMAS | *Gosh, I loved being with him. I just liked him so very much.*

DEVIN | *He made me laugh over and over again. Every time I would go to take a photo, he would make a face which caused he and I to enter the world of giggles.*

KALI | *Kali is a hilarious little princess. She loves to laugh, snuggle, flirt, play, play pranks, run, climb, play with Legos, balls, and do anything else that her older brothers do. She brings a HUGE smile to all whom she encounters and can make a stranger who is having a bad day smile and feel warm and happy. She is amazing in every way.*

JOANNA | *What can I do but smile when I see her? What a character.*

MIKEAL | *He was the sweetest boy but one of the hardest photographs to take. In the end though, it is one of my favorites. His peacefulness was surreal.*

ALIYAH | *Aliyah is sassy and confident. She walks around with a matter-of-fact strut that lets all know she is in charge. And just when you might think she hasn't noticed you, she turns around, and with a smile and a wave with a raspy "hi," she invites you into her moment.*

AVA | *Just look at her. Do I need to say more?*

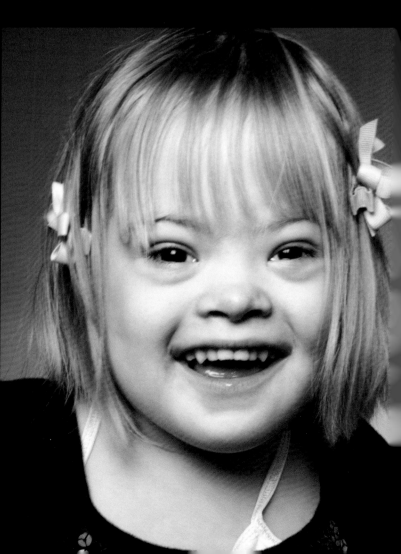

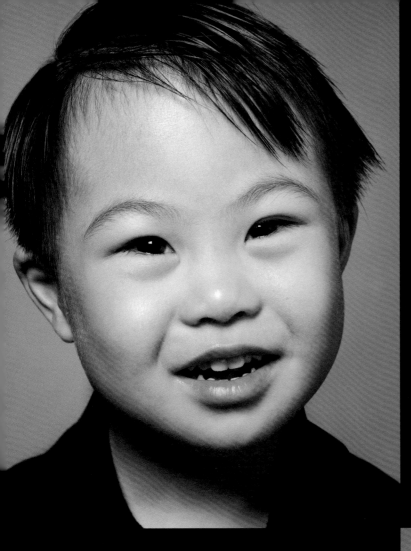

ELLIOTT

Elliott teaches us that one can accomplish great things with a little bit of determination. He continues to exceed our expectations in a multitude of ways on a daily basis.

IRIS

A quick smile from Iris and hearing her say, "Hi Dad!" can instantly erase a workday's worth of frustration. Her simple excitement can motivate me for a week. Her determination and small accomplishments are always with me, allowing me to know that her pure love and happiness is all that is really important in life.

ELIZA

Eliza loves horseback riding and swimming. She keeps bugging me to sign her up for soccer and baseball, and next year she'll get her wish. Currently, her wish is to go into outer space! She's a wonderful daughter, sister and friend – fun, smart, loyal and kind.

Whitney & Randy

By Jagatjoti S. Khalsa

"That may be too hot for you. Lets be careful. I will get some cold water to make the hot chocolate easier for you to drink." A normal dialogue between a father and an impatient daughter. But this was not an average father and daughter. It was perhaps the most beautiful example of love you could witness. A love without neurosis, without angst, without the worry of 'what do I get', without neediness, without anything but love. And it was not just a father and daughter, it was miracle and devotion together, right before us all, to see whether we knew how they arrived here together or not. It was clear.

Fourteen years ago Randy Anderson was a drug addict. He had hit rock bottom so low he took to folding his hands together into prayer pose, and with tears in his eyes he cried out to God for a miracle. Time passed with no miracle but his girlfriend became pregnant. A birth occurred and the miracle happened. A daughter who experiences Down syndrome.

His girlfriend continued her errant ways. Randy soon left the relationship and filed for custody of Whitney. After a short period, the court ruled in favor of Randy and awarded him custody. Even with this daughter she would not, could not, decided not or was unwilling to stop drinking. Eventually she made her choice, the bottle over the baby, and walked away from Whitney over ten years ago. She still lives in the same small town as them and yet has not once come to visit or to know her daughter, now 13-years-old.

Randy became clean. He resurrected his business which has prospered. He recreated his life with this miracle based on love, gratitude, consciousness, grace and passion. He holds his daughter but can let her go. He loves his daughter but can let her be. He serves his daughter but never smothers her. He sings her praises without ever allowing her a big head. He lives for his daughter without losing himself. He loves in the purest form you have ever seen.

He knew upon meeting her that God does answer prayers. And while God answers those prayers, man still has to act. He acts with devotion and love in the rarest way. Look into Whitney's eyes and see the holy woman who healed her father.

My mentor and teacher called me once and said, "To be or not to be – just be." A simple command, a hard act. Randy and Whitney 'just be.' They 'just be' together, they 'just be' in love, they just sit in sacred silence and waves of giggles in a love that can only be an answer to a prayer.

MAKENA & DAD

Makena is empathetic and a good teacher. She recently took a new student under her wing at her preschool and taught her how to sign "Twinkle Twinkle Little Star."

ANANT & PAPA

The name Anant means 'infinite' in the Punjabi language – 'Anant joy, Anant love.'

MEGAN & DAD

Her whole family came to be a part of the shoot one Saturday. But clearly this powerful, loving and amazing girl, was the art director, commissioner and lord over this shoot with a grace and lovingness we should all bring to our work.

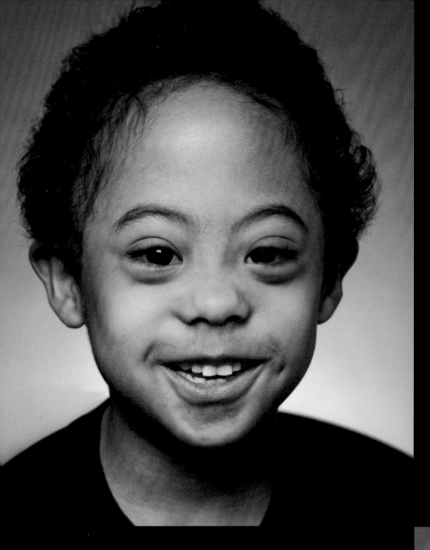

MARC | *Marc is really an amazing boy! He's always been a fighter in life – from the time he was born. He has survived several procedures. He loves going to school and being with other kids. Reading books is one of his favorite things to do.*

DREW | *Drew works so hard every day. He enjoys life and constantly tries to do better. When he laughs, the world (or his world at least) laughs with him.*

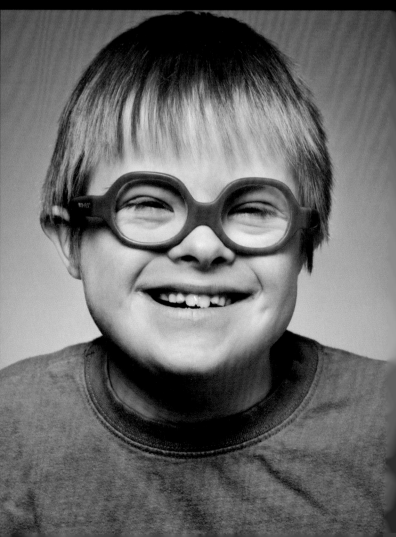

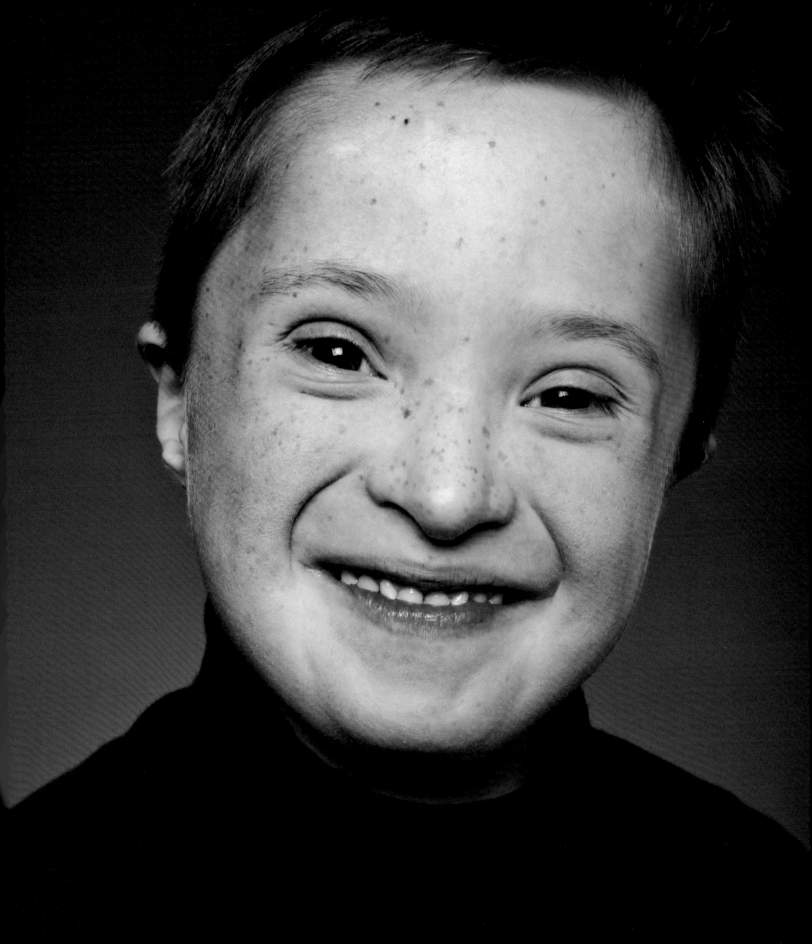

ISAAC | *We look at life through a kaleidoscope of colors thanks to having Isaac in our lives. We rejoice about simple things and accomplishments, such as reading a word and telling time. We blow out candles multiple times because we love to sing the birthday song over and over. We are silly because we can be. We live life in the moment. We have learned the importance of doing things with gusto and passion.*

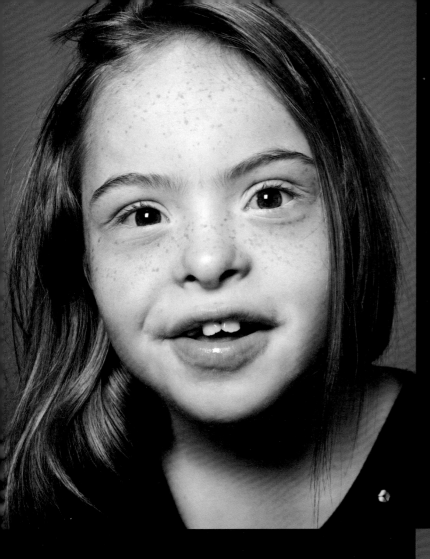

CASSIE | *The amount of love, acceptance and joy Cassie attracts to our lives is constant and immeasurable. She is a human magnet, pulling in all that's good, bringing out the best in everyone who enters her force field.*

KATIE | *She was a commanding spirit. The adage about how a woman can command God on her will was evident in Katie. She seemed capable of making any ocean part on her command.*

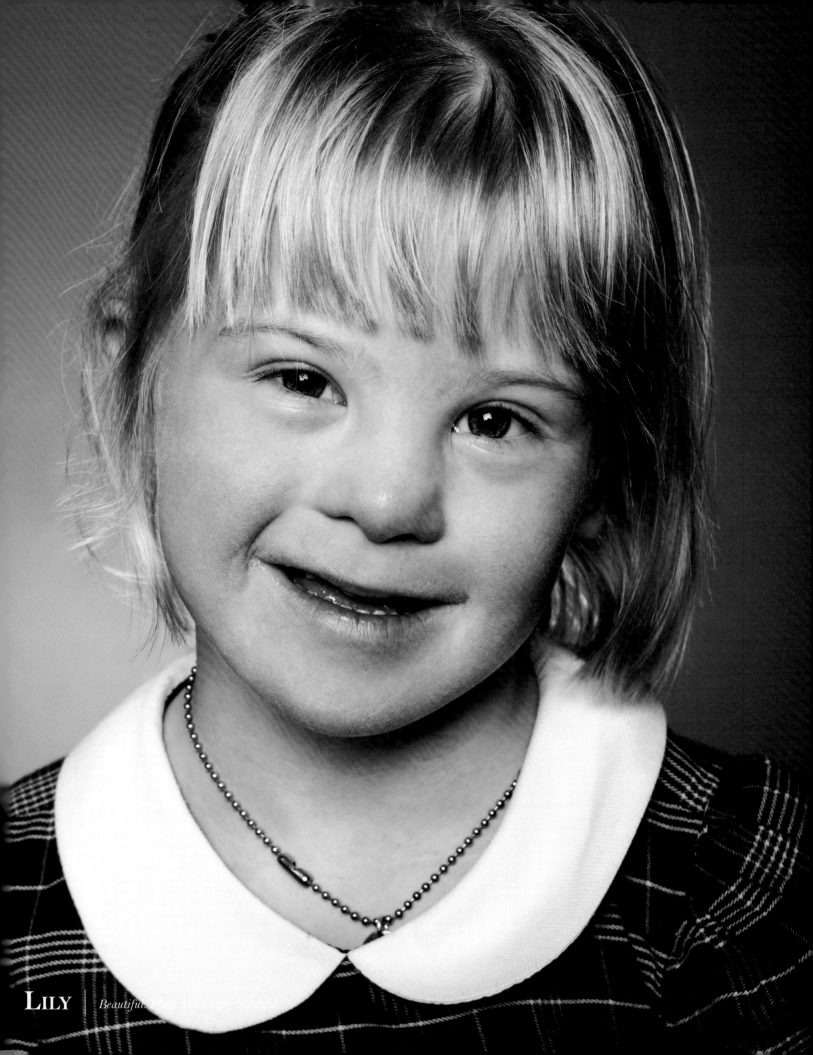

LILY | *Beautiful. Truly and utterly beautiful.*

DYSON | *Oh my gosh. Look at his face.*
He was so, so funny.

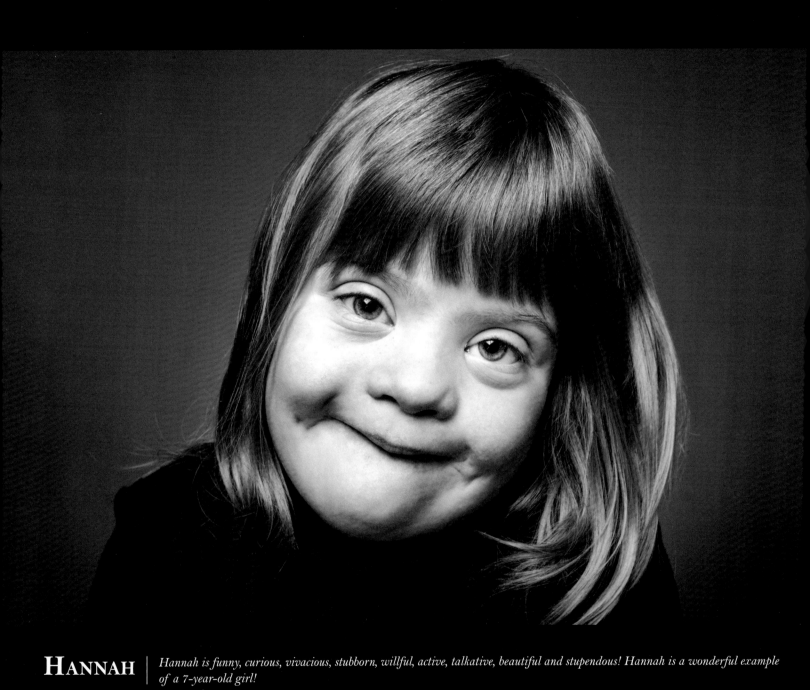

HANNAH | *Hannah is funny, curious, vivacious, stubborn, willful, active, talkative, beautiful and stupendous! Hannah is a wonderful example of a 7-year-old girl!*

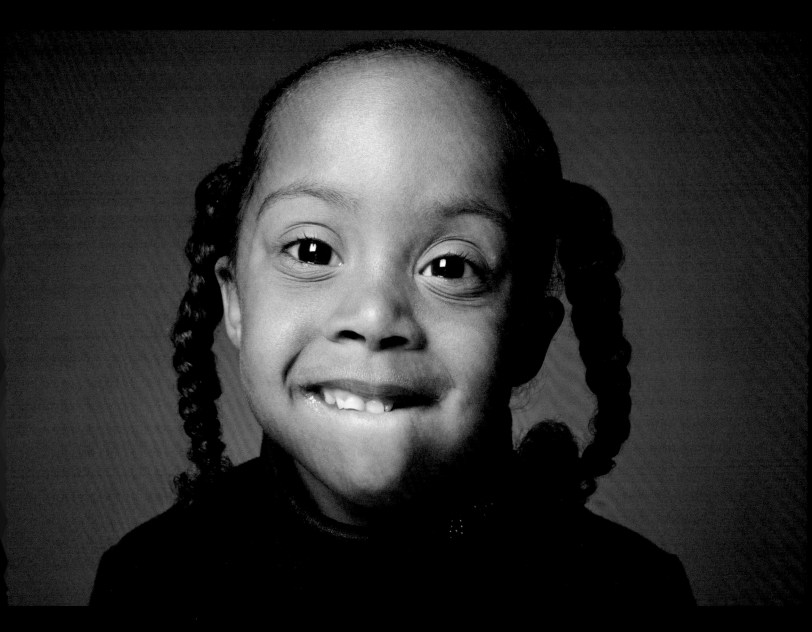

AMOLIA | *She was first to arrive, and upon seeing me for the first time, she ran full-speed into my arms and I was overflowing with her love.*

KEERAN

Keeran loves totally and unconditionally. Pretty great if you ask me. One day I was crying and Keeran came to me, kissed my eyes, wiped my tears and gave me so much love and care. It was a divine moment.

KEIRA

Keira has such a joyful giggle. Her laugh puts an instant smile on her mommy and daddy's face and makes us stop and take in the moment. It's full of pure joy and innocence. It's completely Keira.

JOEY | *Innocently handsome. What a man he is going to be.*

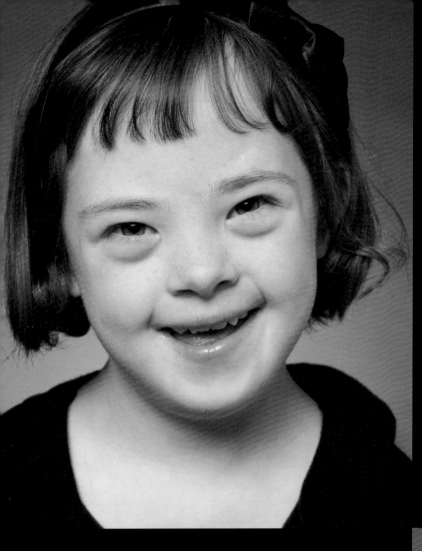

KATELYN

Katelyn is beautiful and full of life. She is always about fun and making people happy. She acted in two movies by age six.

SARAH

Sarah loves to be out and about connecting with people – whether it's performing on a dance team, skiing with Special Olympics, or having coffee on Friday nights with her dad and friends. She always has a smile and hug ready for everyone she meets.

ABIGAIL | *Everyone always tells us to stop staring. But stare at Abigail. Stare at her deeply. Wasn't that amazing.*

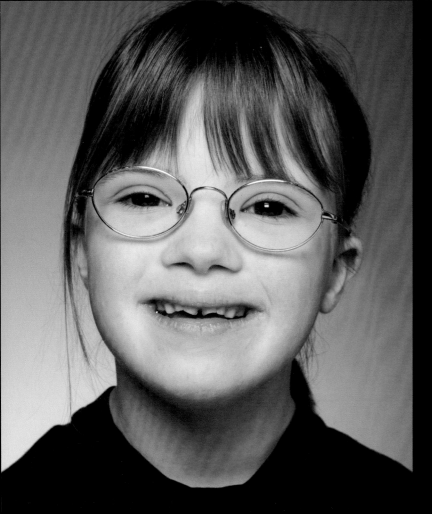

MARISA

Marisa loves trying new things and is always up for adventure. She is a very social girl and enjoys greeting people at our door and talking to everyone she meets when we're out and about. Her spirit is boundless and she puts a smile on the face of almost everyone she meets.

TIM

Tim plays sports like baseball, soccer, tennis and has even tried golf! He is fully included in the third grade. Tim has appeared on "House, Yo Gabba Gabba!" and "Nip Tuck." He has his father's great sense of humor and is very mischievous!

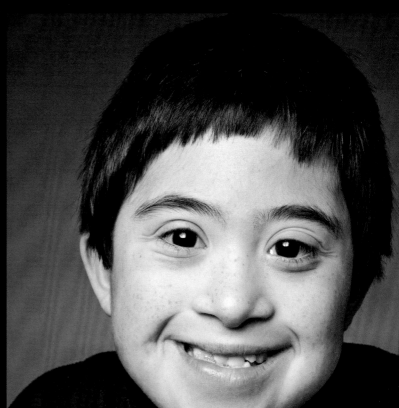

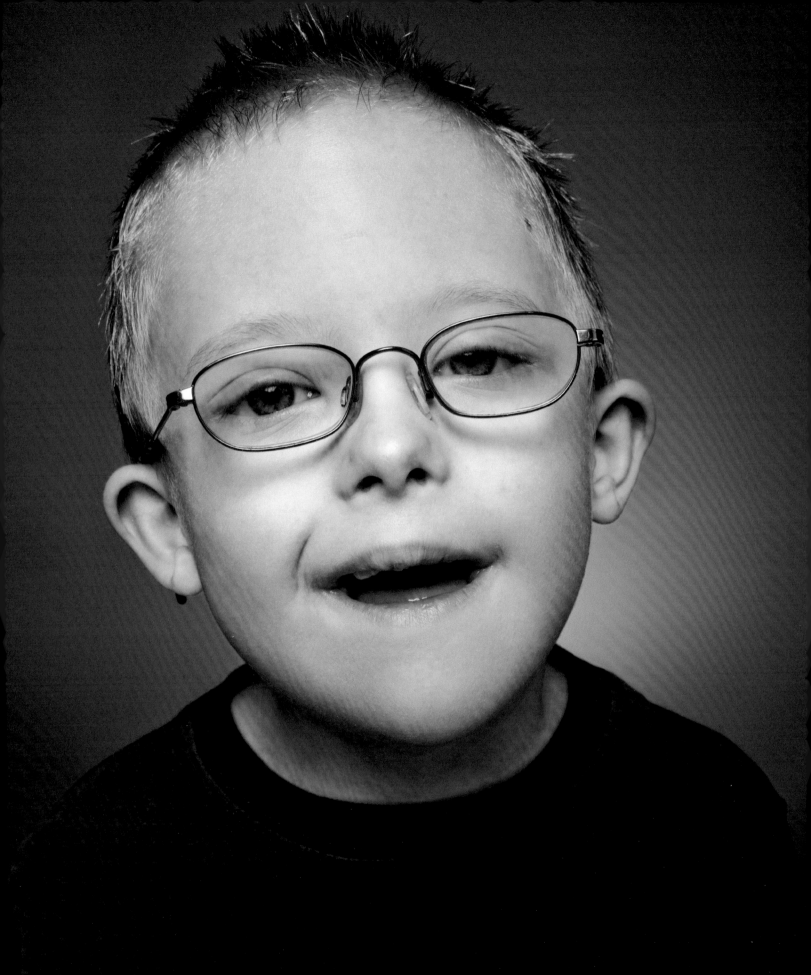

DENNIS | *Dennis is an energetic, athletic and fun-loving boy. He's amazingly handsome, and has a laugh that can stop you in your tracks. His smile lights up a room. He's all boy!*

ELLIE

Love, laughter, joy, beauty....that's Ellie. We know Ellie is here to do great things in this world, and we thank God everyday.

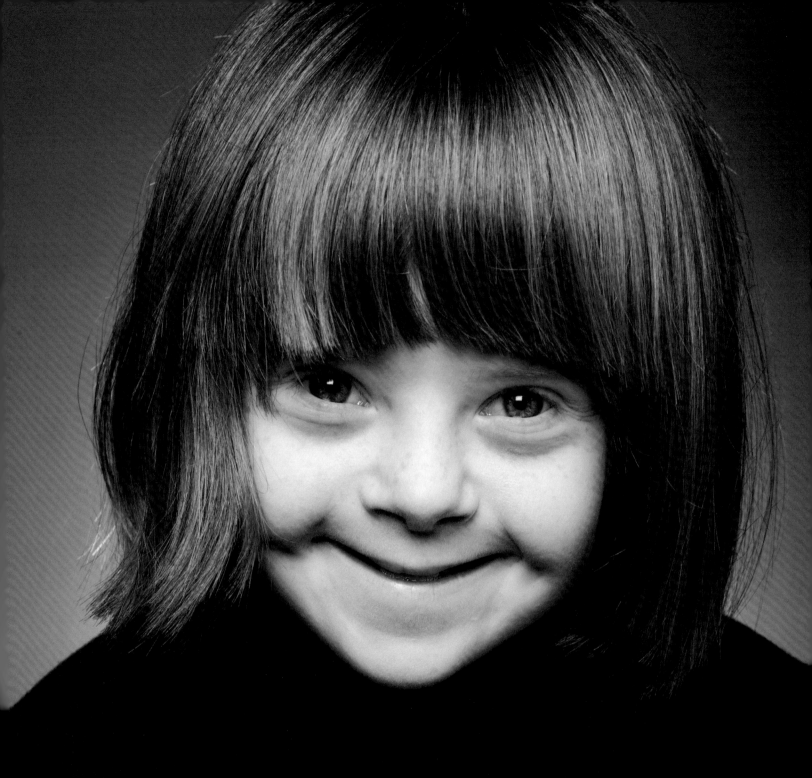

MOLLY | *Molly is the only child with Down syndrome in a general education classroom in her elementary school. She takes piano lessons and sings and acts in an after school program. Molly was in PHAME's production of "Beauty & the Beast" as the only child in the production. She won the most highly coveted award, the Spirit Award, at a one week overnight camp with her brothers last summer.*

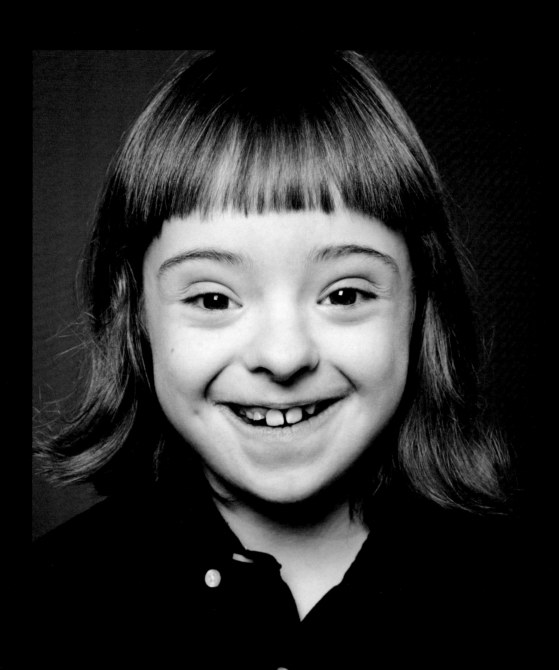

Mary & William

By Jagatjoti S. Khalsa

William and Mary are a typical brother and sister and a love story all-in-one. Theirs is a story of connection, equality and affection. It is a story that seems to be repeated over and over again within the relationships of siblings who I met during my journey with this book.

I met William and Mary at the suggestion of a family friend whose son played with William on a regular basis. William and Mary came to be photographed at my first session.

William is a beautiful boy in every way. Elegance in his movement, loving and present in his words, and gracious and grateful in his interaction with everyone on the set. He looked at Mary, his sister with Down syndrome, with such love and appreciation that within his heart he was who he was because of who she was and their love for one another.

They sat together. They giggled. They laughed a hearty belly laugh. They danced and moved through the photo shoot under the clear directives and dictates

of Mary, who seemed to be art directing with instinct. At a very private and quiet moment, I shot this image. My first for the book. And then, without seeing the image, I was told this story.

William came to his mother, Grace, and said very earnestly and seriously, "Mom, I really wish Mary was not my sister." Somewhat scared and horrified by her son's proclamation, Grace contained herself and asked, "Why William?," to which he replied, "Because then I could marry her when we are older."

William loves Mary with purity, gratitude and honesty. And this seems to be repeated within every set of siblings I have met on my journey. Every brother and sister shares this gratitude and love for one another, not because they are supposed to or feel politically incorrect if they don't, but because this is the experience of their heart.

William and Mary just love each other. It's plain and simple. Not because they should, but because they do.

LOGAN & SISTER

One of the many great things about Logan is that he is very compassionate. If anyone is hurt, crying or just having a bad time he will come over, put his arms around them, pat them gently and say, "It's okay...it's okay."

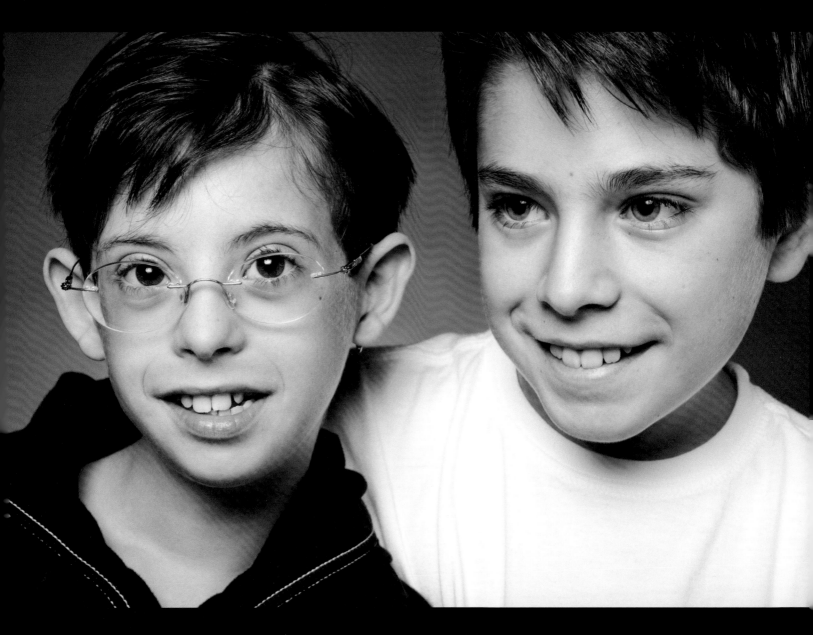

MATTHEW & BROTHER

Matthew is a smart, articulate little boy with a true sense of determination. He lives and loves as if there were no tomorrow. No one in this family works harder than he does. If he wants it, he'll attain it. Matthew observes, learns, and then dictates. Matthew's love is pure, and he asks for nothing in return. We will never be able to teach him as much as he's taught us.

Because of Jesse

By Jagatjoti S. Khalsa

Sixteen years ago Danny Bramson was already a pioneer in the music industry. The great Danny Bramson. Mentored by the venerable Lew Wasserman, he was given his first label at age 25. In a 35-year-period he produced, recorded, signed and created some of the greatest music in history. He managed and put together the ultimate in "mixed tapes" as the head of soundtracks for Warner and enhanced and created our experience with movies, such as *Almost Famous* (think of the "Tiny Dancer" scene on the bus), John Cusack (with the boom box over his head playing *In Your Eyes* by Peter Gabriel), *Jerry McGuire* (when Tom Cruise comes crawling back to his girlfriend), *Austin Powers, Lord of the Rings* and *Mission Impossible* to name a few. He produced the movie *Vanilla Sky* with Tom Cruise and the soundtrack in which Paul McCartney wrote the most incredible song. Some of our greatest movie moments have become even greater by his sensitive and brilliant ear for music.

Sixteen years ago Danny Bramson – the pioneer loved by everyone – was faced with a face full of cold water. Danny and his wife gave birth to a baby boy with Down syndrome. How could this be? Didn't God know who he was? He was Danny Bramson after all. These things did not happen to Danny Bramson. Danny was confused, angry, befuddled, perplexed, hopeless, concerned and scared amongst what must have been hundreds of feelings.

One day while in this space, Danny was driving in Nevada and looked down onto a piece of paper which read 'City of Angels' with a phone number written beneath it. He did not know how it came to be there but figured an assistant must have put it in his car.

Without thought, he pulled over and called the number. There was no reason why he did, and never in the past would he have. On the other end of the line a woman answered and he queried as to what number this was to. He discovered it was a production office to a movie at its end and without a distribution deal but he knew the director. As this process moved along, and with a few more phone calls, Danny Bramson did what he had never, not once in the past, ever done. He agreed to do the music for a movie he had not seen even one frame of.

As he worked on this film, he noticed that this movie mirrored many of the emotions he was having with the birth of his son, Jesse, who had Down syndrome. So he made this film's soundtrack his journey from despair to delight, from hopelessness to happiness, from confusion to hopefulness, from anger to upliftment and to love in its purity. This soundtrack became the most personal of journeys in which the great Danny Bramson processed his emotions from being scared to fearless.

I have told this story to about 50 people, and not only did everyone know this movie, they most specifically recalled being in a dark place in their life and acknowledged that this movie's soundtrack took them on a journey through hardship to healing. Just like it did for Danny Bramson.

Look deeply into the eyes of his son, Jesse, and recall the adage: "Even a quick glance into the eyes of Holy Man can cure the worst ailments."

LARRY

Larry is funny, smart, and would love to have a mustache like his dad. He is always telling everyone, and very proudly, that he looks like his dad. Larry is like clear water, nothing is hidden. He is pure. Larry has the ability to wrap around your heart so easily and he makes you appreciate the little things in life. Larry was chosen as the most valuable player on his soccer team. Larry also has shown a great ability to resolve complex puzzles and video games.

DOMENIQUE

Dominique likes to play soccer, tennis and baseball. He is a charmer and is good at breaking the ice in social situations. He is very social and whenever introduced makes sure the family and others are included in introductions when they are present. Larry is one of his very good friends whom he has known for over five years. They play tennis, swim and do the birthday party scene together. Whenever they see each other they stick together and tackle the world.

ELIZABETH | *Elizabeth is a fully included high school junior. Her fashion sense (as well as hair styling abilities) far outshine many. She has traveled (and shopped) in London and Italy, and her favorite food is sashimi. She wakes each day ready to go no matter what hurdles the day before brought her.*

LAUREN

At an awards ceremony, actress Lauren Potter (Glee), reached out and held my hand after she received her award. As I prepared to receive mine, lost in thought, she said, "it is going to be okay, you will do great!" I realized that it was not just this awards ceremony she was speaking of. We share a special love, and I think she shares this love with everyone she meets.

BRANDON

Brandon has a quiet confidence intermingled with a great sense of humor. He gives his all in everything he does and never gives up until he reaches success. He doesn't follow others but rather sets his own standards and has a true sense of right verses wrong. He'll never say an ill word about another, he loves the unloved and he has the right equipment to touch lives that need to be touched.

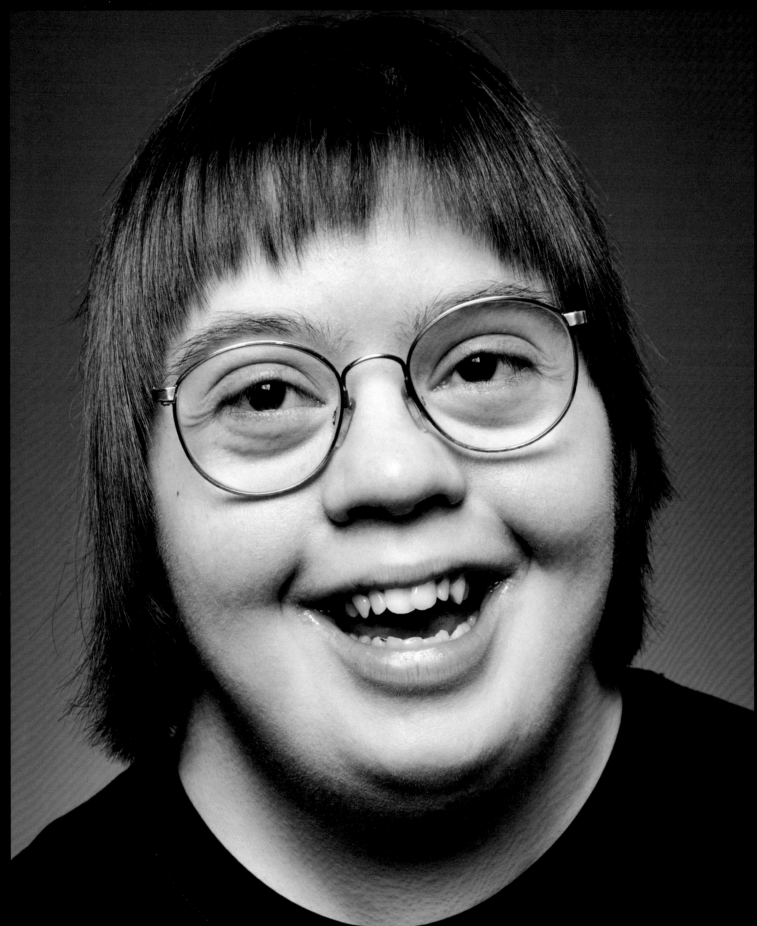

HEATHER | *I saw her at the grocery store and I knew this book would be incomplete without her.*

SAID | *Said is a very sweet and caring young man. He always has a big hug for his good friends. He loves to sing and dance. Music moves his soul. He's also a regular athlete with Special Olympics, participating in swimming, power lifting and floor hockey.*

CALEY | *Elegant, beautiful and radiant. She was incredibly funny and brought such a great energy to our session. What an incredible young woman whose family lineage is connected to President Adams.*

KARA | *It seems too soft to say she was nice, but she was. She was the purest, sweetest, kindest form of nice.*

EMILY | *Emily lives in her own simplified world, yet she is so in-tune with everything around her. Her insights continually amaze me. She can bring her own personality, quirky humor and joy to every situation. You can count on her to bring her own perspective on everything, as nothing escapes her notice.*

KATIE | *Katie has been riding the Tri Met Lift bus independently to and from her three office jobs for almost four years. She takes great pride in her work and prefers working to taking a vacation. She also attends art and music classes at Phame Academy, participates in several sports in Special Olympics and loves dancing and cheerleading.*

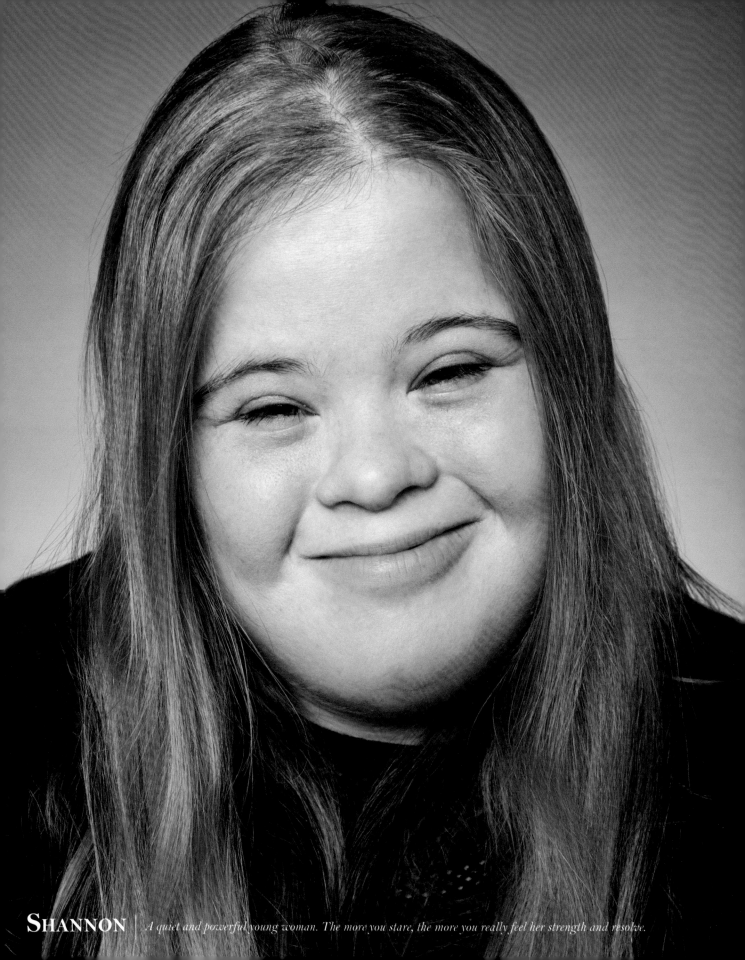

SHANNON | *A quiet and powerful young woman. The more you stare, the more you really feel her strength and resolve.*

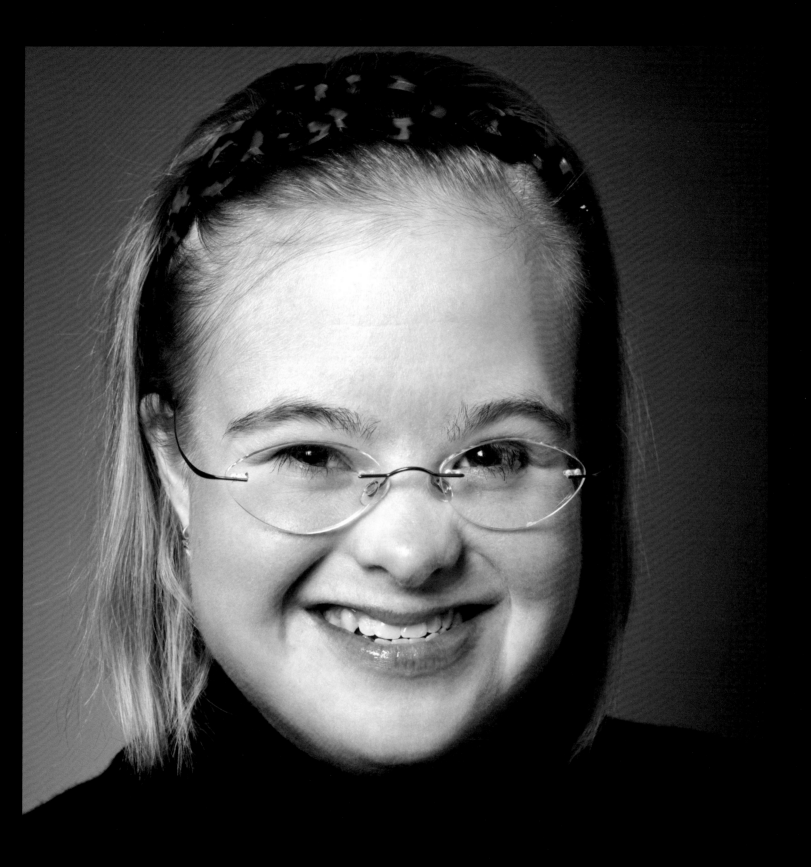

KATE | *She was so elegant and graceful. She carried herself like a modern day princess.*

PARTH

Measured, calm, present and strong. Parth was a pillar of strength — strength of character, intellect, heart and the very best example of whom I would want by my side if ever I needed someone to trust.

JARED

Plain and simply, Jared is the coolest person I have ever met. He walked with a saunter, projection and impact. You knew you were in the presence of a great athlete (more gold and silver medals than you could count) and more importantly, a great man.

LAZ D | *Rap artist. Complete character. Strong minded. Strong willed. Incredible talent. A little intimidating. Rap music? "I have the mind for it, an ear for it and the voice for it."*

Jim & Sharon

By Sharon Stone

When I was fourteen I was called for a babysitting job. Two kids, if I remember correctly, which I would get paid fifty cents an hour to watch – one little girl and her older brother. They were nine and eleven at the time. It seemed great. They lived just down the street in a very nice house across from the golf course. My parents said yes.

When I got there I noticed that the boy, the older one, was pretty big for his age, had a big head and was loud. The girl was very sweet and very, very kind. She was helping her brother a lot and looking at me like she was watching TV.

Her parents didn't say anything special about their son – just what he liked to eat and when they would be back – and then they left. I began to realize just how special he was.

He was very intuitive and had a kind of psychic aware-ness of what was going on. He was hilarious and inventive, and incredibly strong. I quickly realized that I had to be careful because he was crafty and a prankster and would lock me in a closet or put water in his parents gas tank if I took my eyes off of him for long. But if I got into the groove, he would show me a world of wonder that no other child or adult had ever revealed before or since. He was a seer.

Jim knows.

There is a truth to his mind that is based in an undeniable clarity that cannot be broken, stolen or corrupted. It just is. Purity – solid, clean, durable purity – flows through him and it is wise and deep and hilarious as only the truth can be. His sister is his *other* – his transformed other traveler. To have been the protected and the protector is an amazing journey and it was a privilege to see them grow up and out and through together.

She is a special education teacher now. A leader and still a follower. They are still guides for those who know only the truth. The rare and delicate flowers in God's gentle garden. This was the best job I ever had until I was given my own job of Mother.

Jim reminds us all of how he locked Sharon in the closet and stares at us with that "cat got the mouse" smartness.

JULIE | *One joke after another. She was so magnificently funny and she was an accomplished actress. An all around incredible woman.*

KEVIN | *Kevin is an active guy ready for adventure on a moment's notice. He has done minor and background roles for TV and movies, and loves acting on stage. Kevin attended a film-making program for special needs students and would like a job as part of a film-making team. He also enjoys editing his own videos and giving them to friends.*

C.J. | *C.J. is like a movie star. He has this charisma and star-quality which is evident in his eyes and his smile.*

JAMIE | *She was the easiest person to spend time with, as she made me and the rest of us laugh so much, and yet at the same time was in no way making herself a clown in doing so.*

JASON | *Jason is the funniest fellow ever. Even just a hint of him makes me laugh a great chant.*

TIM | *Sure this picture is serious and contemplative. But watching him with his girlfriends (ex and current) showed such a capacity to love I am befuddled even today.*

J.T. | *When he hit the set, a star was reborn. One-hundred poses which kept me in hysterics. This one spoke of his power to move an army of souls.*

Love is Home

By John McGinley, Actor & Father of Max

The opportunity to empower a child born with Down syndrome is a great gift. That is a hard one to see at first. I know! In fact, at first, the whole thing is just way too much to even wrap one's head around. And it is mainly because we are afraid. We are terrified!

The fact of the matter is that people go out of their way to get rid of or abort babies who will be born with Down syndrome. And yet, here you are holding this child whose 21st chromosome his tripled! (And, what the hell does all that mean anyway?) We haven't a clue. So, we are afraid. We are scared!

Here is what is scary.

Inadequate integrating of oxygen into the blood. Microscopic holes in the heart. The neo-natal intensive care unit. Sleep apnea. Sleep study tests. Infantile seizures. Oxygen canisters. Appropriate preservation responses. Occupational therapy. Hippo-therapy. Cranial-sacral therapy. Fine motor skills. Gross motor skills. Chat rooms. Conferences. Board of Education Advocates. Vitamin interventions. Dietary restrictions. Infection susceptibilities. Orthopedics. Degenerative disorders. Alzheimer's Disease. Low muscle tone. Post secondary education. Regional Centers. Bullies! Exclusion...

And how on earth do we overcome these fears? How is one to organize this phenomenal bombardment of new and profoundly disorienting input? One thousand times: "HOW?"

That is the challenge. But it is all the biggest opportunity that you may ever be presented with. It is a chance to be truly great at something. It is a once in a lifetime offer to amount to more than just that person staring back at you in the mirror every morning. You are in a position to love. You get to care about someone who must have your care. You get to trump fear by preserving glimpses of joy!

Now, we will always be afraid of this, that and the other thing. But it is almost impossible to live in fear when we are actively engaged in giving love and pursuing joy.

And what trumps being afraid?

Swimming in a pool. Laps! Reading a sentence. Reading a paragraph. Reading the whole book! Shooting hoops. Throwing the ball for the dogs. Surfing the Net. Memorizing the entire "Wiggles" cannon. Putting on puppet shows. Hitting a ball off the tee. Playing songs on the piano. Constructing whole railway lines. (And building stories around the finished construction.) Doing your homework – every last bit of it! Walking the bride down the isle. Dialing people up on the telephone. Breaking your own pinball world's record. Hanging ornaments on the Christmas tree. Pitching off the mound. Being super-gentle with a new born baby. Actually helping other kids on the trampoline. Watering the tree that you helped plant. Singing duets in key and in the groove! Scoring two goals in the soccer game. Hugging the life right out of your father!

Whenever possible – in gestures, activities, initiatives, protocols, encouragements, discipline, games, work and even during the quiet time – we are in a position to cultivate joy and nurture love. You get to be "that guy." You get to be "that parent!" The one who was scared to death because he had a kid with Down syndrome. The one who was also strong enough to elevate out of fear and into love.

Being afraid is real and it can be paralyzing. But it does not have a chance when home is love and love is home!"

BLAIR

Blair loves photography. He makes our family chase sunsets while he looks for the best location to take the shot. Blair will walk further for a sunset than a meal. He also likes to make slide shows of photos of his friends. He will sit at his computer night after night arranging and re-arranging the photos to make sure they work just right with the music he selects. He is creative in every way.

BLAIR & SUSIE

Blair loves. He has loved Susie for over six years. He understands how to love a woman. He was raised with our six cousins who came to be a part of our family after the deaths of my brother and sister-in-law. These women in his life have raised the bar, teaching him patience and understanding. He can also give a great back rub.

John Kelting, Jr.

By Caroline Kobin

A truly gifted prodigy of social connectedness and creativity. I met John during transition in my own life. A helper, revisiting my vocational choice.

I never expected to find such a unique, real, lovely, brotherly soul and a renewed hope for the human soul. John is the simplicity in life. His straightforward understanding and straight shooting attitude reinforce my own skills, that although sometimes dismissed as a clinician, remind me that human connection is not all about "language". Our purpose is to recognize ourselves as connected to the world and to be, to see what happens. This is a truly advanced perspective to achieve, considering our anxiety filled environment. An acceptance of all and self that is truly peaceful and Buddhist.

My connection with John began with *Terminator 2*. We both said, "That's my favorite movie!" at the same time. I was impressed with John's artistic talent, but his spirit was most captivating. It turns out that we share many of the same interests, both enjoy painting and drawing our interpretation of movie heros and beauty, both enjoy coffee, people and Starbucks. John is the person who you go out with in the community and meet ten people who say, "you look familiar, how do I know you?" He is the one who, knowing that I think Robert Pattinson is hot, brings me the posters from US magazine that he has already painted and says, "Don't tell your husband, you can put it up in the closet." He is proof that a limited vocabulary can actually enhance a relationship.

How to describe?

A whirl of his paint brush; his tongue peeking out the right side of his mouth in concentration; a tilt of his head; his infamous Terminator-style leather jacket (rain or shine); his characteristic, "AWESOME!", "NO WAY!", or the way he says, "YOU'RE KIDDING!" with a giggle and a waggle of his eyebrows; the simple and sincere emotions, "did you forget about me?"; the ease at which he can shed a tear or make your day; his endearing text messages that, although in secret code, nonetheless remind you of his desire for human connection and your own warm fuzzy that someone is thinking of you; his perfect celebrity bedhead about which he says, "I'm making it longer like Edward's" (in reference to *Twilight*); his collection of movies ranging from *Hannah Montana* to Oscar winners like *The Aviator*; his need to carry around his laptop wherever he goes to be online; his perfect flirtation with women, "What's your name?", "I have an aunt named ......"; his enjoyment for everything new; his enthusiasm of all movies; "THAT WAS AMAZING!"; his perfect pitch Michael Jackson scream coupled with the disco hand movement when we are rocking out in the car.

What more can I say? Keep being yourself, dude.

CHERISH

Cherish loved having her photograph taken almost as much as I loved taking it.
Once she sat down, she locked into my eyes and took me on an amazing journey.

KAREN

I was awestruck to be meeting THE Karen Gaffney. She has crossed Lake Tahoe, Boston Harbor, Alcatraz (four times) and the English Channel, all swimming. And if you meet her, you will see that her grace and heart are even bigger accomplishments. And if you spend time with her, you will see that her love, gratitude and service to our world is the best of her accomplishments.

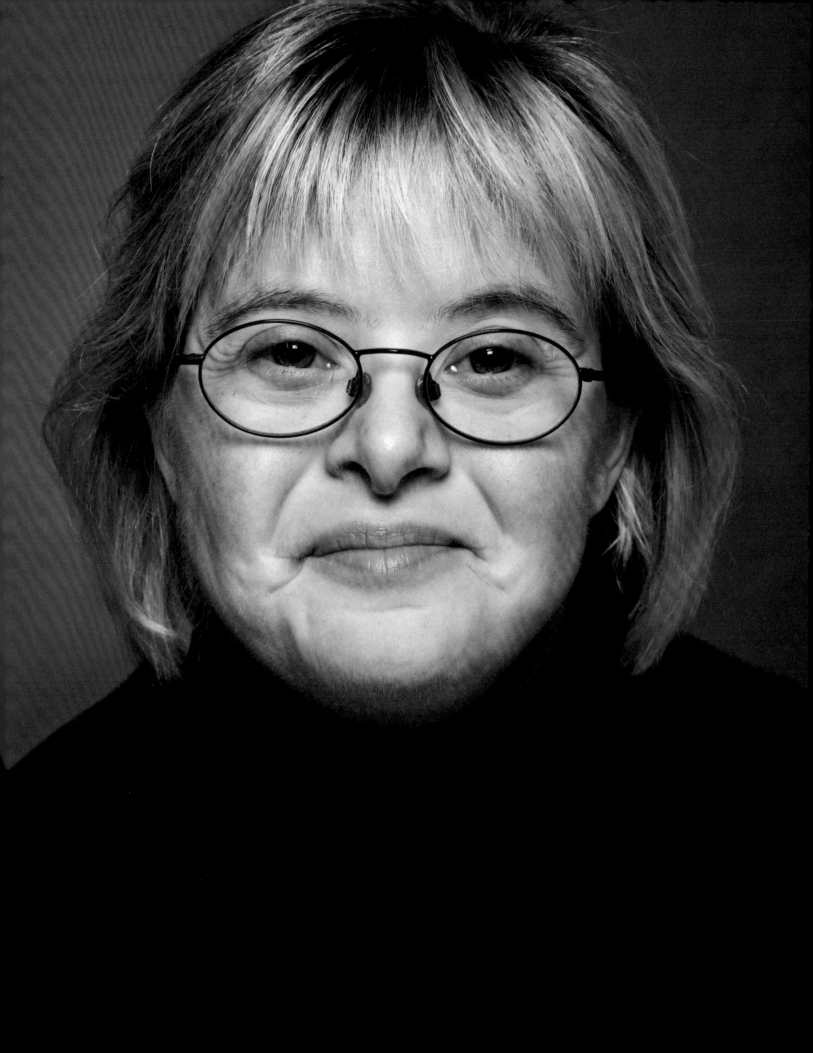

MARCIA | *Quiet yet full of laughter. Contained yet full of life. She had that subtle power and strength you knew you could count on*

SUSIE | *What can I say? Simply one of the most beautiful and loving women I have ever known. And to watch the shared love with Blair puts Shakespearean Sonnets to shame.*

Jim & His Dad

By Jagatjoti S. Khalsa

"Dad," Jim says to address his father, Richard, who is now 79-years-old as we have dinner. My heart warms and a flood love overtakes me as I hear this sweet sound. I have never heard such a sound. The melliferous sound brings such an overwhelming feeling to me – it will be forever anchored in my heart.

"Dad," with the perfect innocence, love, honor, respect and connection. The sound brings tears to my eyes even as I write this, "Dad." Not once has the sound left my lips as it leaves his each time. This is a 49-year-old man – a man with his own apartment and great job for the past twenty years. A true man – open hearted, trusting, loving and in full-blossom. He does not operate with any feelings of saying "Dad" and feeling little, weak or insecure. He just loves like you have never heard. There should be a recording we all listen to with this sacred sound. The simplest word with the most incredible feeling. I know many people talk about loving their father. Many profess commitment, respect and passionate conviction to how much they love their parents and their fathers. But in my years, I have never heard it sound like this.

Maybe Jim knows or maybe he doesn't. Maybe he cares or maybe he doesn't. Maybe he has never even had it cross his mind. But many children of this generation with Down syndrome were cast away or institutionalized. They were marginalized and sent to homes. They were out of sight to be out of mind. Many passed away in their 20's, as that was the life expectancy in this generation. Many parents and our society did not know what to do with them, so away they went. No socialization. No care. No life. Nothing. But not this family. Not Jim's dad.

What did he know of a child with Down syndrome? What did he know about how to serve, love and honor this child of his? What help, assistance or support group existed? Here they were, two parents with a child different from the others.

I will tell you what he did. He loved him, served him, spoke with him and honored him. He built him up. And together they loved each other. Richard loved Jim. And when Jim says "Dad" it is a celestial purity which we are all taught and few of us realize. Think of the things we are taught in school, in church, at temple, in books and every other place. Now combine them all together and you have this sound of "Dad."

This journey is not over. Jim's generation is the first one to outlive their parents. Imagine the stress of that on Richard and his wife. But you would not know it as they hold each other and Jim says "Dad." And Richard replies with the heartiest, most loving nod and eyes of love. This is his son and this is Jim's "Dad."

KRISTINE

Kristine loves her job – and her paychecks! She sees each day as an exciting adventure. She was the first person with Down syndrome to graduate from her high school and she is a proud of her membership in SAG.

ROBIN & SISTER | *Happy and accomplished without bragging. She was so incredible. Actress, grocery chain employee, sister, friend and joyous addition to every environment she entered.*

CHRISTINE & MOM

Love is a Potion

By Jagatjoti S. Khalsa

"Love is a Potion" is what Melissa Riggio taught anyone fortunate enough to listen. A radiant, loving angel of a woman who lit up every room she entered, Melissa wrote and sang songs with a selfless and soul-serving grace one could see in her eyes and in the affect she had on her community. She gave her parents love, warmth and upliftment.

I stumbled upon this picture when I began my journey at the suggestion of Karen Gaffney. I opened her website and was blown away. Her words "Love is a Potion" spoke to the essence of this project, and in its four simple words, spoke volumes. Imagine if we took love every day, consciously, thoughtfully and aggressively and placed it into our work, directed it to our spouse's hand, our hugs with our child, our communication with co-workers, and into a simple request for our morning coffee. What if we offered it as guidance to those who were struggling, and added it to our toothbrushes each morning when we brushed our teeth and washed our face? Imagine how our lives would look

today had we sat at the feet of this wise woman who stirred a little "love potion" into every word, every action and every look she gave.

Imagine a life in which you added this potion to everything you do. Imagine that life. Can you imagine wanting to live any other way?

We use mantra to train our mind away from nonsense and to imbue it with grace. "Love is a Potion" is one of those mantras. It was not given to us by a PhD or scholar, nor was it discovered in ancient texts or scripture. It was not given to us on a tablet by Moses or dictated by Buddha. Yet it echoes with the essential nature of all traditions of wisdom across time.

Here is a young woman who gives us a mantra for the Aquarian age. "Love is a Potion" is a simple, repeatable statement to carry in our hearts and minds — a main ingredient in the recipe of a more loving, joyful daily life.

Gratitude

I am not sure what really made me embark on this journey, to write and photograph this book, but within every fiber of me I am grateful. This experience has become a living and breathing meditation for me. Every cell in my body wishes that I could do nothing but photograph, speak about, speak to, serve and be around this community. Everyday in which I was scheduled to work on this project turned out to be my best day. Every hug I received when working on this project turned out to be the most incredible hug. Every letter, email, call and discussion became the most incredible experience and one which would be forever anchored in my heart. If our lives are a mosaic of our experiences and the people we meet, few things have had such an influence as the Down syndrome community has had on me.

It was not only the people within the Down syndrome community who I am grateful to for their impact on me and this project. So many incredible people came just in time to commit their hearts, consciousness, love and grace to serve this project. Not once did anyone ask me what was in it for them. The project began with a conversation with my agent, Jan Miller's assistant, Annabelle. She was the first person who listened to my vision, and with the widest smile and with incomprehensible support she encouraged my effort. And thus began the string of people's support. Jan Miller did not require to finish the second half of the sentence before she asked what she could do to help.

I walked next door from my office and spoke with a young and incredibly talented photographer and post production genius named Darren Setter. Not only did we become friends, but I could not have done this book and project without his partnership. He is a humble, thoughtful and open-hearted man who very quietly moves through our world and leaves behind greatness without concern or need for recognition.

As I needed to present this project to share with the community and with partners, I designed and developed my own website. And then, through a friend, I met this designer, Annette Thurston. One day we went for a walk and she said I'll help you with this project and created the book's website without charge. Then I received an email in the wee hours of the morning which said, "All teasing aside, your photographs are beautiful and I feel privileged to be designing your book." It was I who felt privileged to be by her side, learning how to do selfless service with one's heart.

When the project began I wanted to take videos of the shoots and capture some of the incredible stories I was experiencing. I asked my friend, Lubosh Cech, for his company, Naked River Films, to shoot one of the sessions. From there on, he donated all of his time and resources to start producing a documentary which makes everyone cry because of the love he captured and the love he puts into his work. You can feel what an incredible man he is as soon as you see the first frame of his work.

So many people offered to help as I needed subjects. They went out of their way and introduced me to people within the community so I could share my vision including Gail Williamson, the executive director of Down Syndrome Association of Los Angeles. The Gaffney family helped me with my first photo shoot with the incredible Karen Gaffney.

Jos Tervo, Teresa Gruber, mother of Brandon and Elizabeth Brown, and Janet Levin, parents of Eliza, and many others all helped me find subjects, recommended and trusted me with their friends, and everyone in the community who came to be a part of something without any knowledge of me and with a great trust that I would present them in ways full of respect, love and honor. I have never experienced a community who could open their trusting arms to a stranger.

One of the people I was introduced to was Sarah Schleider, the VP of Marketing and Communication for NDSS. She instantly become one of my favorite people. Everyone should have the chance to be around this incredible woman. She worked without question, without fail and with so much grace, appreciation and strength. I was humbled to work by her side. She helped form a partnership with NDSS, assisted with marketing and PR efforts, partnered with me in every possible way and was the smartest, most talented marketing professional I have ever had the pleasure to serve. Each phone call humbled me more to her incredible strength, power and unfailing passion to serve this community.

We also had incredible people show up just to be a part of the photo shoots including Chris Jackson and Out of Frame Studios from LA; Brooke Narragon and Dawne Alane-Kelmenson, both of who came and spent sixteen hours serving everyone in every way during our LA shoots; Dan Ostrander who arranged everything with us in Portland and, like Darren, was irreplaceable.

There are so many more friends I have to thank – my wife and daughter who loved this project from the beginning and who, even more than me, sees God in all. My business partner and friend, David Howitt, who upon seeing the first images knew we had become part of something special. Sharon Stone who made not only an incredible contribution to the book by sharing her story and being photographed with her friend and now mine, the Burkhardts, but helped me gain confidence that as a photographer I could hold my own in this project. While he wouldn't know this, Louis Randa (The Peace Abbey and Life Experience School), invited me many years ago to attend his morning meeting around the Peace Keeper's Table. From there I first saw this community in a new light. To my hundreds of dear friends, thousands of Facebook friends, and just about everyone who crossed this project and loved it so purely, gratefully and supportively – it is your project as much as it is mine.

Credits

The beautiful quotes and statements with each photograph were provide by the people below. They are all family members, parents and siblings, caregivers and friends. Where none were provided, Jagatjoti provided his inspiration from the shoot.

Kevin Ewing by Kathy Ewing
Elianah Hoff by Jay & Deanne Hoff
Christine Young by Dana Young
Blair Williamson by Gail Williamson
Susie Schallert by Mary Schallert
Malea Smith by Chrystal Smith
Matthew Von Der Ahe by Emmy Von Der Ahe
Tyler Wetsch by Carrie Wetsch
Katelyn Reed by Kelly Reed
Dominique Torres by Mark Torres
Larry Charles Baker III by Sandra Baker
Olivia Hawkins by Christine Hawkins
Marc Williams by Ezell Williams
Shannon Dieriex by Theresa Dieriex
Jamie Brewer by Cindy Brewer
Kristine Johnson by Sharon Johnson
Sophia Flores by Rosa Flores
Tim Borquez by Fred & Monica Borquez
Emily Boccignone by Carolyn Boccignone
Elliott Song by Marissa & Young-Sae Song
Cassie Elizabeth Wootan by Lynda & Chris
  & proud brothers, Scott & Max Wootan
Felicie Allamanche by Francoise & Eric Allamanche
Said Padellan by Nicole Kim

Elizabeth Allan by Amy & Ryan Lopez
Brandon Gruber by Teresa Gruber
Sarah Schellenberg by Rick & Michelle Schellenberg
Aliyah Tovar by Susan Tovar
Eliza Brown-Lewin by Liz Brown & Janet Lewin
Drew Scarlett by Anita & Mark
Molly Murphey by Celia & Jerry
Nicole Williams by Nancy & Rick
Keeran Kannan by Segar & Debra
Anna Paschal by Janine Paschal
Logan Scharosch by John & Lisa
Katie Godoy by Steve & Cheri Godoy
Makena Olsen by Nancy Korf & Clint Olsen
Isaac Hawthorne by Robert & Wendy Hawthorne
Kali Levy by Ariel & Debbie Levy
Marisa Szwarc by Sara Szwarc
Laz D by Marcy
Katie Carlsen by Rosemary & Bernie
Iris Tervo by Jos Tervo
Hannah Galati by Mari & Joe Galati
Anant by Shannon Chawla
Dennis Reese by Ken & Christy Reese
Megan Schiedler by Paula Schiedler

Photo Credits:
Melissa Riggio, *Love is a Potion* by Peter Farago
John & Max McGinely by Leah Hodgget

Book & Website Design: Annette Thurston - www.athurston.com

Your Great Story

People with Down syndrome are doing great things and they are contributing to society in many great ways. We are *down* with educating the world that people with Down syndrome should be valued citizens and their accomplishments should be celebrated. Won't you join us?

Tell us who you are *down* with and join forces with the National Down Syndrome Society's "My Great Story" campaign to honor and celebrate the 400,000 Americans with Down syndrome. Share your pictures and words of who you are *down* with.

If you have Down syndrome, tell us about your dreams, talents and aspirations, or if you know someone who has Down syndrome, tell us how they have inspired you.

Visit **www.ndss.org/stories** to share your great story.

The Other Person is You { foundation}

The Other Person is You {*foundation*} is a nonprofit foundation devoted to creating compassion, consciousness and awareness that we are all one. This is the first project from the foundation. The foundation convenes conferences, produces motion and still images in the form of books, web content, documentary films, and live and recorded music, and awards grants to other charitable organizations, all with the purpose of creating an experience for the individual to have their hearts and eyes opened and their souls reminded that before them - The Other Person is You. To learn more about our projects and for more information, visit **www.theotherpersonisyou.org.**

Facts About Down Syndrome

- Down syndrome occurs when an individual has three, rather than two, copies of the 21st chromosome. This additional genetic material alters the course of development and causes the characteristics associated with Down syndrome.

- Down syndrome is the most commonly occurring chromosomal condition. One in every 733 babies is born with Down syndrome.

- There are more than 400,000 people living with Down syndrome in the United States.

- Down syndrome occurs in people of all races and economic levels.

- The incidence of births of children with Down syndrome increases with the age of the mother. But due to higher fertility rates in younger women, 80% of children with Down syndrome are born to women under 35 years of age.

- People with Down syndrome have an increased risk for certain medical conditions such as congenital heart defects, respiratory and hearing problems, Alzheimer's disease, childhood leukemia, and thyroid conditions. Many of these conditions are now treatable, so most people with Down syndrome lead healthy lives.

- A few of the common physical traits of Down syndrome are low muscle tone, small stature, an upward slant to the eyes, and a single deep crease across the center of the palm. Every person with Down syndrome is a unique individual and may possess these characteristics to different degrees or not at all.

- Life expectancy for people with Down syndrome has increased dramatically in recent decades - from 25 in 1983 to 60 today.

- People with Down syndrome attend school, work, participate in decisions that affect them, and contribute to society in many wonderful ways.

- All people with Down syndrome experience cognitive delays, but the effect is usually mild to moderate and is not indicative of the many strengths and talents that each individual possesses.

- Quality educational programs, a stimulating home environment, good health care, and positive support from family, friends and the community enable people with Down syndrome to develop their full potential and lead fulfilling lives.